Markham

206L

Making a New Home
IN AMERICA

by Maxine B. Rosenberg
illustrated with photographs by George Ancona

Lothrop, Lee & Shepard Books
New York

To Sharon—my editor, mentor, and friend
—M.B.R.

To Claudio Edinger
—G.A.

Text copyright © 1986 by Maxine B. Rosenberg
Illustrations copyright © 1986 by George Ancona
All rights reserved. No part of this book may be reproduced or
utilized in any form or by any means, electronic or mechanical,
including photocopying, recording or by any information storage
and retrieval system, without permission in writing from the
Publisher. Inquiries should be addressed to Lothrop, Lee &
Shepard Books, a division of William Morrow & Company, Inc.,
1350 Avenue of the Americas, New York, New York 10019. Printed in the
United States of America. First Edition
2   3   4   5   6   7   8   9   10

Library of Congress Cataloging in Publication Data
Rosenberg, Maxine B.
   Making a new home in America.
   Summary: Text and photographs present the stories of five
children who have come to the United States as immigrants or
resident aliens from Japan, Cuba, India, Guyana, and Vietnam.
   1. United States—Emigration and immigration—Juvenile
literature. [1. United States—Emigration and immigration]
I. Ancona, George, ill. II. Title.
JV6450.R67   1986   325.73   85-11642
ISBN 0-688-05824-8   ISBN 0-688-05825-6 (lib. bdg.)

When Jiro was seven years old, he lived in Tokyo, Japan, a city across the Pacific Ocean from the United States.

Six mornings a week, no matter what the weather, he'd put his heavy book bag on his back and set off for the forty-minute walk to his school. There he would work in class all day, with only a break for lunch: hot soup and *nimono*, Japanese meat and vegetables, which he ate with chopsticks. At home he would study, often for two or three hours. Then

he'd have dinner in a small room that served as his family's kitchen, living, and dining room. By eight o'clock Jiro would be asleep on his *futon*, or floor mat, next to his younger sister, Naoko. Much later Jiro's father would return from work. Like most Japanese children, Jiro only saw his father for a few minutes each morning.

A year ago, when Jiro was eight, he and his family moved to the United States. Now weekday mornings he gets on a school bus with a few books and a ham-and-cheese sandwich. In his pocket is a baseball, which he uses during his class's two recesses. At three o'clock Jiro either goes to gymnastics or visits a friend. That leaves enough time for him to do his one hour of homework before his father comes home. At 7:00 P.M. the family eats together in their large dining room. Often Jiro uses a fork and knife. By eight-thirty he is asleep in a bed in his own room.

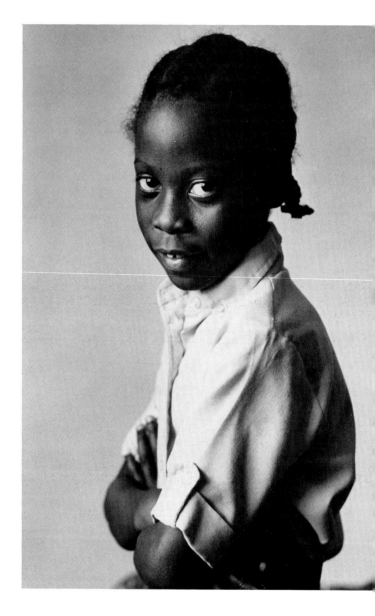

Like Jiro, Carmen, age seven, Dasiely, age nine, and Farah, age eight, are all newcomers to the United States. Although each is from a different country, they have much in common as recent arrivals to America. And they are not alone. Every year almost one million people come to America to live.

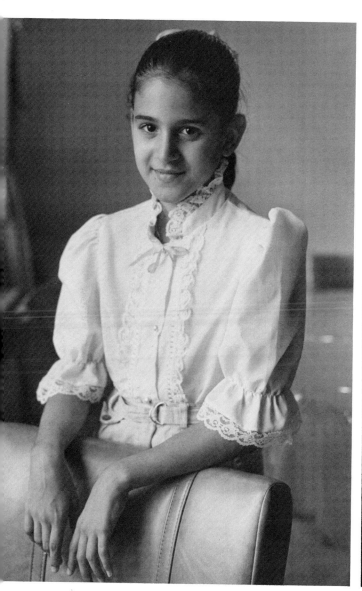 

There are many reasons for this. Sometimes the chance for better schooling brings people here. Sometimes a job makes the move necessary. Farah's and Jiro's fathers, for example, brought their families when their work was transferred to this country. When it is finished, five years from now, the families will return to their homes, Farah's in India and Jiro's in Japan.

Most people who come to live in the United States, however, plan to stay. They are immigrants—people who have come from another country to make their home here. Six out of every one hundred persons in the United States are immigrants.

Some immigrants are looking for greater freedom—to practice their religion, perhaps, or to write or talk about ideas that may be punished or forbidden in their own countries. When Dasiely and her family left Cuba a year and a half ago, she knew they could never return. That's because her father had angered the Cuban government by speaking against its leaders. Not only was his job taken away then, but also police were always watching the family, especially after they said they wanted to come to the United States. It took twelve years for that wish to be granted.

Other immigrants leave their home countries to escape war or to seek a better life. Carmen and her mother, for instance, came here two years ago from Guyana, South America, so that Carmen's mother could get a good education and earn more money.

For whatever reasons they leave and however long they stay, newcomers usually discover that America holds some surprises for them.

"I thought I'd see Indians riding in the street," says Jiro, "but they were only on TV."

And Farah was certain the United States was one big, crowded city. "Was I amazed when we moved to a house in the country, with a garden," she says. All she needed, then, was a friend.

In the beginning, though, friends are not always easy to find. Even if newcomers arrive speaking English, the way Farah and Carmen did, language can make fitting in difficult.

"Every time I'd go out to play," says Carmen, "someone made fun of my accent." When this happened, Carmen would ask her mother if she could go back to Guyana to be with the children with whom she had grown up.

Jiro arrived in America speaking only Japanese. Although he knew he would be returning to Japan in a few years, he tried to make friends here. But not knowing or understanding English well made it hard. Popular words or sayings were especially troublesome. "Kids would call my Japanese sneakers 'wicked' or 'fresh,'" says Jiro. "I thought they were teasing, and so instead of saying, 'Thank you,' I'd get angry."

School can also seem lonely and frustrating when there are language problems. For example, a newcomer to this country may be too embarrassed to ask a question and end up doing the wrong assignment. Even worse, he or she may be held back a year in school, to make learning easier. This happened to Jiro, and it made him think he was stupid.

"Everyone laughed at me, even though I was working hard," he says, recalling what it was like being in second grade instead of third. Having a first-grade reader made the experience even worse.

For Jiro, reading also meant learning a whole new alphabet that was totally different from the Japanese characters he knew so well. Because he felt low about himself, Jiro was often noisy and did not listen, which annoyed his classsmates. "But," he defends himself, "how could I listen when I couldn't understand what anyone was saying?"

Not being able to speak the language also made Dasiely feel left out and lonesome. Because she spoke Spanish, she had no one to talk to at recess. And after school, she would play only with her brother, Doony. "I missed my friend Nadia, who was in Cuba," Dasiely says with a sigh.

Language is not the only new experience. Moving to a new country also means learning new ways of living and new customs. Sometimes this can be frightening and confusing.

For Farah, who was used to servants laundering her clothes in the Indian rivers and streams, turning on the washing machine herself was scary.

And when Jiro first came to America, he could not understand why most people keep their shoes on indoors or why there are no public bathrooms. In Japan he had always worn slippers in the house, and if he needed a toilet when he was away from home, there were signs for them posted on almost every street.

However, as Jiro soon discovered, it isn't always necessary to give up old customs. Many times Americans are eager to share them. Now, when Jiro puts on slippers at home and eats his meal with chopsticks, his friends do the same.

Farah and her family have also found a way to continue part of their culture in their new country. Members of a small religious group called Parsees, they located a nearby temple where they can pray. For their special holidays, Farah's mother still prepares an Indian feast, and family members wear their traditional clothing.

There are many changes, though, that most newcomers are happy to make. Food is one example.

"We eat hamburgers for supper, not rice and beans as in Cuba," says Dasiely, "but pizza and spaghetti are what I like best." Most newcomers share Dasiely's enthusiasm for these American favorites.

For Carmen it's a special treat to look at the shelves and shelves of toys in American stores. "You couldn't find many toys in Guyana," she says, "and if somebody ever got one, he never let anyone touch it."

Now Carmen's mother works as a dietician's aide in a hospital and goes to school at night so she can get an even better job. Sometimes she surprises Carmen with a doll or book. What's more, after having lived in a small house with lots of relatives in Guyana and then with relatives in America for a year and a half, they now have their own apartment. They are especially proud of their new furniture and large color TV.

Dasiely's father also has a job, and her family has its own apartment too. What particularly impresses Dasiely is living in a building with an elevator and having two cars. "Cuban apartment houses didn't have elevators, even if they had five floors," she says. And in Cuba only government workers drove cars.

More than anything, though, if children have never seen it, snow seems to excite them most. Farah thought it was so beautiful, she wanted to eat it. And she couldn't wait to try ice skating. Since where she lived in India is hot and has only rainy and dry seasons, Farah had not been on ice before.

At Carmen's school they let the children sleigh-ride at recess. Then later, at home, she and her aunt built a snowman. Carmen didn't remember when she had enjoyed herself more.

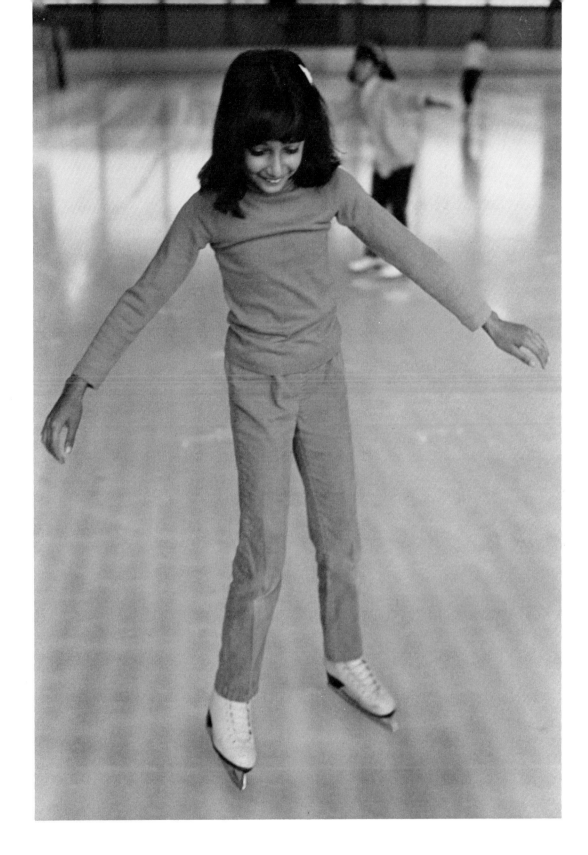

Another pleasant surprise for young newcomers is school. "In India there were forty-five girls in my class, and I had to wear a uniform with itchy high socks," Farah says, wrinkling her nose. "I like the smaller classes here, with boys and girls together. And it's nice dressing the way I want."

When Jiro's teacher asked him to tell the class about Japan, he brought in *kendama*, a Japanese ball game, and some picture books. He also introduced the children to a new Japanese word each day.

To help him improve his English, he was assigned a special person outside of class to teach him the language, just as Dasiely has been taught. "I can read and write terrific," Dasiely boasts, "but I don't like being taken out of art."

Now that she's more familiar with English, Dasiely, like many children new to this country, looks forward to going to school every morning. And in America, she no longer worries about being watched or that her house will be searched while the family is away.

As each year passes, newcomers feel more a part of this country and more comfortable with its ways. Although Jiro knows he will return to Japan someday, he confesses now he'd rather stay here forever. Since this won't happen, Jiro attends Japanese school every Saturday so he won't forget his native language.

It's different for Dasiely and Carmen, who are planning to become American citizens. Once the families have lived here for five years, the parents will apply for citizenship papers for

everyone. Then, as soon as the grown-ups pass a test for
English language and United States history, the family will go
to court together and be sworn in as Americans.

"I'm glad I'm living here," says Carmen, "except sometimes I get lonely for my cousins in Guyana." Last year, in fact, Carmen and her aunt returned to South America for a visit.

"It was great seeing everyone," Carmen says, beaming, "but I was happy to come home to America."

Epilogue: Tuan's Story

Ten years ago a Vietnamese boy named Tuan unexpectedly came to the United States. His parents, realizing their country was losing a war, were able to escape with the family just in time. All they took with them were the clothes they were wearing.

Tuan was six then. He had never ridden in a car, and he knew little about America. When his family arrived here, they had no money, no jobs, and no home. Tuan's father was the only one who spoke English.

With the help of a local church and townspeople, the family started a new life. They were given a small house with furniture, clothes, and food. And a job was found for Tuan's father—gardening for $2.75 an hour. It was not much money to support a family of seven, but at least it was a start.

Today Tuan's father is the supervisor of a printing company. He used to ride a bike to work; now he goes by automobile. From their own savings and with help from neighbors and churches, the family bought a home of their own. And Tuan has already begun dreaming about buying a car for himself.

More important, Tuan admits, was the day six months ago when he became an American citizen. "As a child I didn't know what freedom meant. Now I can appreciate having no one tell me how to live my life," he says.

When he gets older, Tuan hopes to become a systems analyst. He would also like to return to Vietnam to visit his uncle and grandfather. "But America is my home," he confides. "That's where I want to stay."

About the Author and the Photographer

Making a New Home in America is the fourth book written by Maxine B. Rosenberg and illustrated with photographs by George Ancona. The books they have produced together clearly prove that they are a remarkable photo-documentary team. In a starred review of *Being Adopted*, their second book, *School Library Journal* noted, "This exceptional look at an increasingly common type of adoption will be reassuring for children who are adopted and enlightening for those who aren't." With the addition of each new book, it is apparent that the essential ingredient that distinguishes a Rosenberg/Ancona photo essay is their ability to express the honest feelings of their subjects in a way that is both informative and reassuring to young readers. Their other books, *My Friend Leslie*, about a small girl with multiple handicaps, and *Being a Twin/Having a Twin*, also have been praised for these exceptional qualities.

Ms. Rosenberg's sensitivity to the feelings and experiences that separate people and the human needs that bring them together has been honed by her years of teaching gifted and handicapped children, as well as by her ongoing education as mother of four. Her Korean-born adopted daughter, Karin, became a naturalized citizen of the United States at the age of three. Now a full-time writer, Ms. Rosenberg lives in Briarcliff, New York.

George Ancona grew up in the colorful world of New York's Coney Island, the son of Mexican-born parents. His many books, several of which he has written himself, reflect his infectious energy, his good humor, and his keen, penetrating eye for the human side of people and events. The father of six children, Mr. Ancona lives in Stony Point, New York.